Memoir of Grace
(Children of the Cross)

Aqif Shahzad

En Route Books and Media, LLC
Saint Louis, MO

United States of America

⊕*ENROUTE*
Make the time

En Route Books and Media, LLC

5705 Rhodes Avenue

St. Louis, MO 63109

Contact us at

contactus@enroutebooksandmedia.com

Cover credit: Mary Kloska

Copyright © 2022 Aqif Shahzad

ISBN-13: 978-1-956715-31-6

Library of Congress Control Number: 2022932937

Mary Elizabeth Kloska

Dedication

I dedicate this book to all the persecuted Christians, children of the Cross in Pakistan and throughout the world, and to Our Lady Mother Mary, and to Baby Jesus, who is our Savior. I see this baby Savior in all children of the Cross, and his cross brings me closer to the persecuted Christians.

Word of Thanks

- First of all, I am grateful to my God, who chose me for this sacred and important mission here in the Middle East and throughout the world.

- I am grateful to Our Lady, whose presence in my life always gives me joy and the feeling of being loved and accepted the way I am.

- I am very thankful for Mary Kloska, who is the reason for this mission in the Middle East and throughout the world. She has given life, light, hope, peace, and joy through her life and books in my country and all over the world. I am thankful to God for her wisdom and love for the people. Mary, thank you very much for giving me permission to translate your life-giving books. God bless you, your parents, and the whole family even more!

- I am really very grateful to Mary Kloska, who has painted the cover page of this book, Our Lady of Pakistan.

- I am very grateful, from the depth of my heart, to Dr. Sebastian Mahfood, OP. The book in your hands is the result of his love, concern, and support. He has played a key role in helping this ministry to flourish. I would love to mention here that it was his initiative to ask me to write this book. Thank you very much, Dr. Sebastian Mahfood. God bless you more.

- I am also thankful to all the Children of the Cross, teachers, women groups, new converts, missionaries who have encouraged me and are always with me in this sacred and life-giving mission. I am very grateful to my participants in the seminars, workshops, churches, and groups of all sizes who have taught me a lot.

- I am very grateful to my family, my wife and daughter. Their support and encouragement means a lot to me. My mother, brothers, sisters, sisters-in-law, brothers-in-law, and all nieces and nephews.

Table of Contents

Preface

Our Lady of Pakistan

While praying for the people of Pakistan and Afghanistan in October of 2021, this image came to my mind of Our Lady of Pakistan.

She is a radiant light of love shining in the darkness of suffering in Pakistan, and She is spreading Her Light from Pakistan throughout the Middle East. If Jesus is our Sun, Mary is our Moon reflecting His Light. She is also called the 'Star of the Sea' to help guide us on our path towards heaven. It is especially fitting to include these two symbols on the right in this icon of Our Lady of Pakistan as they are also present on the Pakistani flag. The purple rose on the left on this icon is a symbol of the hidden fruit She is also bearing in Afghanistan. It is hidden (as is represented by the dark purple flower) and seemingly separate from Our Lady, and yet it is She who is bearing this fruit in the neighboring country. Our Lady is surrounded by all sorts of roses–dark purple ones representing hidden souls, white ones representing the innocent ones, red and pink representing those who suffer–and Her Heart is resting in a nest of deep red roses representing those martyrs who have been killed for their faith. The 'Fiat' on Her dress is red–for the Fiat of Her people in Pakistan has had to be one united to the Blood of Her Son Jesus Crucified. Her heart is pierced by the sword of sorrow and has four nails representing the nails in each of Jesus' Hands and Feet. The very center of Her Heart has a white rose representing the purest fruit that comes from Her Heart. Golden Light surrounds Her as rays of heavenly love radiate out from Her. Yet hidden between the rays are dark blue stars representing all the hidden souls in Pakistan radiating Her Light in the shadows of that land.

May Our Lady continue to protect, enlighten, comfort, and strengthen Her special chosen children in Pakistan!

Alleluia! Fiat!

Mary Kloska +

Introduction

A short reflection. *Memoir of Grace (Children of the Cross)* depicts my feelings of gratitude. This book helps us to see the wonders and miracles that God has performed through Mary Kloska's books. We will look at how her books have given light, life, and healing to wounded and persecuted Christians. This memoir also reflects my personal experience with God. I am happy to share my personal life journey that shows how God chose me for this ministry with the Children of the Cross.

Christianity in Pakistan is always in search of justice, freedom, and peace. It is a bitter reality that many times in Pakistan, Christians are treated badly because of their religion. Young girls are forced to marry and change their religion. They are physically raped and put to death. Low ranking jobs, such as janitors (sweepers), are assigned to Christians only. This religious discrimination is very clear.

Children and even adults have lost their Christian identity. Women have lost their dignity. People are experiencing hopelessness, darkness, injustice, and uncertainty. This memoir explains this situation in detail.

Most importantly, this memoir helps us to understand how the "Children of the Cross" ministry has changed the lives of many. We will read how this ministry is giving hope, light, justice, and life to the people.

We will come to know how a simple translation work has turned into a ministry. You will read how God has chosen and picked a simple person from a village and used him for his glory throughout the world.

And, of course, the reading of this book will help us to know how a woman of God, Mary Kloska, has touched and changed the lives of many here in Pakistan, Afghanistan, and all over the world. A woman from the first world has touched the hearts of the third world with her pure and sacred love.

So, let's begin to read this life-giving journey….

Chapter 1

"But I chose you…"

God chose Mary to be the mother of Jesus, our savior, and to be hope, life, light, and peace for those who are rejected and living in pain. Jesus chose me to be with Him to visit all those who are living in uncertainty, experiencing death every day, being raped and put to death, having no meaning in life. I completely believe that it is not me, but that it is He who has chosen me. It is through His love and grace that He chose me. I am not worthy to be chosen, but He saw the image and likeness of His father in me. I am created in the image and likeness of God, but my deeds are not up to His merit, yet he chose me.

He also chose my mother to give me birth. My mother is a very simple woman, a true and faithful lover of Our Lady. My mother lost her husband (my father) early. She never shared that story with me, but I am sure this journey of life would have been tough for her. She was not highly educated yet raised her children according to the will of God. I always experience God in her and her in God. She is a prayerful person. Now, even though she is physically very weak, she is spiritually well-rooted. My spiritual roots and energy come from her.

Now, I can imagine and feel her screams when she gave birth to me. I imagine that when she saw me her screams and pain turned into joy and comfort. That time, maybe, I could not feel her pain, but now I do. My mother, Our Lady, all the mothers and Jesus shared through their painful experience that there is no new life without pain. In my life, I also had countless painful experiences. And these painful experiences made me sensitive and attentive to the pain of others.

A lot of sufferings and pain surround me every day. Young girls are raped. Innocent people are put to death because of their religion. The dignity of womanhood is not respected. Forced conversions and marriages are taking place. Children are dying physically and spiritually. I always prayed to God to reveal the purpose (mission) of my life. I spent years in prayers to have an answer. And now "Children of the Cross" is the answer. To be the voice of the voiceless is the answer. To be the light in the darkness is the answer. To be life amidst uncertainty and death is the answer. To do the will of God is the answer, "Truly I tell you, whatever you did for one of the least of these brothers and sisters of mine, you did for me." (Matthew 25:40)

Early life

The LORD said to me, "I chose you before I gave you life, and before you were born I selected you to be a prophet to the nations." I answered, "Sovereign LORD, I don't know how to speak; I am too young." But the LORD said to me, "Do not say that you are too young, but go to the people I send you to, and tell them everything I command you to say. Do not be afraid of them, for I will be with you to protect you. I, the LORD, have spoken!" Then the LORD reached out, touched my lips, and said to me, "Listen, I am giving you the words you must speak." (Jeremiah 1: 4-9)

My name is Aqif Shahzad, and I belong to Pakistan. I was born in a village, situated close to Sahiwal. I have three brothers and two sisters. I am the youngest in my family. After the death of my father, my mother played a significant and heart-touching role in our family and in my personal life. My life in the village was simple and deeply connected with trees, fields, animals, flowers, and with other simple people like us.

I always woke up early in the morning hearing my mother praying out loud for the whole family. Her prayer never missed any name. She was a true lover of Our Lady. Though she did not know exactly how to say the Rosary (like she did not know all the mysteries and even did not know on what day which mysteries are recited), she never forgot to pray it. My love, faith, and devotion to Our Lady has roots in my mother's devotion to her.

Early life in the village was simple and pure. Getting up early in the morning, going to school, and playing in the evening was a normal routine. I had never been outstanding or extraordinary as a student, but I loved and enjoyed my studies.

National Days, Easter, Christmas, and unexpected holidays from school were the main celebrations. It gave me pleasure to see more or less everyone sitting in the streets, under the trees in the afternoon in hot summer. In winter, people used to sit around the fire in families and chat for a long time. These two seasons (extreme heat and cold) always brought people close to one another. People were well aware of what was happening in the lives of one another.

I was born in 1978, and I never left the village until 1993, for these few years, the village was my whole world. At the age of 15, for the first time I left my village.

I can write much more about my early life happily but here I am going to focus on other things, the graces and miracles of my life. It is enough for the reader to understand about my childhood, that the memory of my childhood, even now, leaves me with joyful tears.

Life with Franciscans (OFM)

"Let us begin again for up until now we have done nothing" (St. Francis)

As I mentioned in the introduction that my early upbringing was only in the village, I never had exposure to the outside world. At the age of 15 was the first time I left my village and family. I left it to join the Franciscans. Moving from a very small village to a huge, big city (Lahore) was something extraordinary happening in my life. I missed fields, animals, trees, and simplicity in this city.

But I was very happy to see once again this simplicity and integration with creation when I joined the Franciscans. I stayed about eight years with the Franciscans as a religious brother but now (even though I am not part of that fraternity), I claim to have grown into more of a Franciscan. I simply love St. Francis and do my best to follow his teaching through my deeds and words. St. Francis helped me to see God in all and all in God.

After completing my four years postulancy, I went to Sri Lanka for my Novitiate. Now from a village to a city and from this city to Sri Lanka was a time of learning. In Sri Lanka I did my Novitiate with the Philippine community. During my Novitiate, I was under the influence of two cultures, the Sri Lankan and the Filipino. After completing my Novitiate, I came back to Karachi for a two-year religious course. Then in the eighth year, I had to discontinue with them. Here it is worth mentioning that when I left them, I thought I lost St. Francis, but after a few years I really discovered that it is only now that I have met him (St. Francis) in person. This will not be an exaggeration if I say that St. Francis introduced me to Jesus. I touched the wounds of Jesus in Francis' wounds.

Now, again, a lot could be shared about these eight fruitful and fertile years. These eight years enhanced and gave depth to my understanding of how to meet Jesus in ordinary people. During this life, I did my pastoral work among special children and adults. Though this was a very difficult time, it was always full of love and God's blessing. I also did my pastoral work in Sindh, a place with a different and rich culture. Even in this place, people are connected with creation and seek God in His creation. Jesus' words to St. Francis: ***"Come build my Church; it's falling to ruin"*** are very significant to me. I feel these words are also said to me. These days, when Christian people are being persecuted because of their religion, priests are in trouble, very small girls are being raped, and girls are forced to change their religion, remind me of the falling church. I am called by God to build this church anew, through good news, news of hope, love, peace, and light.

Life with Columbans

"If you want to know the creator, know creation." (St. Columban)

Columbans are a group of priests and lay missionaries who serve throughout the world including Pakistan. They have been serving here in Pakistan for more than thirty years. I worked with them for about five years. JPIC was one of the offices run by Columbans in Pakistan. JPIC stands for Justice, Peace, Integrity of Creation. This office assignment was to spread awareness about ecological issues and our relationship with God. I was the main facilitator in this office. I conducted workshops throughout Pakistan in all provinces. Our main theme was to respect, love, and care about God's universe.

This job gave me the opportunity to see the whole of Pakistan, and I loved this job because I could meet different people every day. During this job I came to know different cultures and religions of Pakistan. This job also gave me an opportunity to see the religious and economic condition of our Christian brothers and sisters.

After spending about three years, I was sent to Ireland for a couple of weeks for a retreat. This retreat became a source of energy, wisdom, and love.

A few years ago, I thought that life in a small village, in a big city, then throughout my country, in Sri Lanka and even in Ireland is just a coincidence. I felt this all happened because this is the requirement of my job to move from one place to another.

But now I feel that was God's plan to choose and pick me from a small village and put me into places to form me and appoint me to the people of hopelessness, darkness, hatred, and betrayal in order to bring them hope, light, love, peace, and trust.

Teaching is my passion

It was he who "gave gifts to people"; he appointed some to be apostles, others to be prophets, others to be evangelists, others to be pastors and teachers. (Ephesians 4:11)

Teaching is my passion and a gift from God. I am called to be a teacher. This is a fact that teaching is in my blood. My father was a teacher, and all my brothers and sisters are teachers, too. God has given me many exposures and opportunities to learn so that I can teach well. I have taught in schools, in seminars, in workshops, to individuals and groups. I have been teaching (and of course learning) for the last twenty four years. This is my call to be a teacher. It will not be wrong if I say that I never thought to be a teacher. But with the passage of time, I discovered that God has chosen me from my mother's womb to teach. Now I feel that because of this passion (teaching) I am able to preach as well. When teaching and preaching become one, under God's will, then miracles take place. My listeners always acknowledged and appreciated me as a teacher.

Teaching requires faithfulness and of course skills and openness to learn. I always tell my listeners that I am not there to teach them but to learn and explore with them. My teaching is always based on small personal examples and experience. I teach from my heart, and I feel this touches the heart of a listener.

As I shared earlier, since I was born in a village I found animals, fields, flowers, birds, trees, and grass around me. This was God's creation. My place of learning is this creation. Creation is my teacher. She taught me to be a teacher. My learning and teaching exposures and experiences are from this universe. I discovered God in this universe.

"But ask the animals, and they will teach you, or the birds in the sky, and they will tell you; or speak to the earth, and it will teach you, or let the fish in the sea inform you." (Job 12:7-8)

Translations

"Then he said to his disciples, 'The harvest is plentiful but the workers are few.'" (Mt.9:37)

Translation is another gift of God bestowed to me. When I left the friary, I started translating books as a source of income. This work not only helped me to earn a living but also enlightened me. In the beginning, I was doing this work for the sake of money. Later, I realised that there are many insightful books in English, but in my country the majority of the people cannot read English well. So, then I decided to continue this work not only to help me, but also to help others.

Up till now I have translated twenty-five books. These books gave me earning, learning, wisdom, insights, experiences, exposures, and much more. When I started translating **"Holiness of Womanhood"** (written by Mary Kloska), however, I found that this translation gave me something no other translation project had yet done, namely grace (blessing), which brought me closer to God. This book helped me to know more about God. Every sentence of this book enhanced my understanding about the holiness of womanhood. This book explained how a woman is born in the image and likeness of God. This book helped me to see God in woman and woman in God. *Indeed, the translation of this book completely changed my life. God, who was preparing and forming me for some mission, revealed the mission through this book*

The
Holiness
of **Womanhood**
Mary Kloska

نسوانیت کا تقدس
میری کلوسکہ

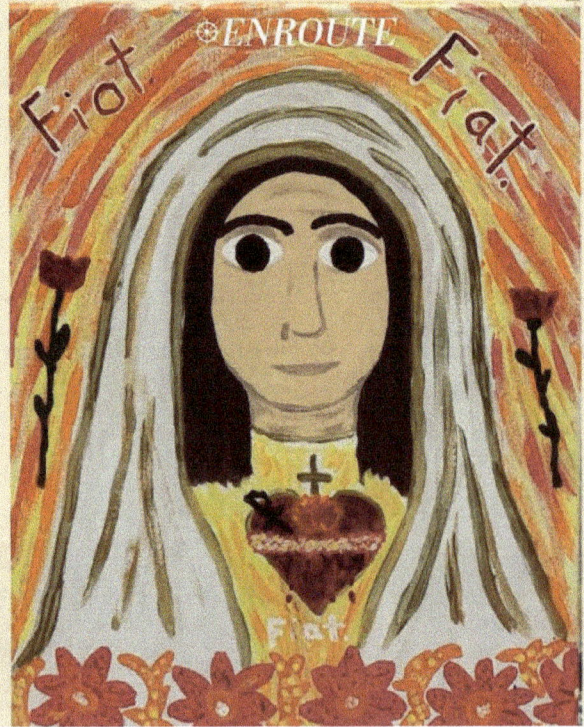

Chapter 2

Children of the Cross: A Children's Apostolate of Prayer for Priests and Persecuted Christians

How God turned a simple translation work into a Ministry and Mission!

I have translated many books, and all of these books have given me knowledge. When I started translating Mary Kloska's books, however, the work really gave me not only knowledge but also personal experience with God. I never thought that translation of her books would lead me to a mission that is already planned by God.

Mary Kloska (many know her very well already, but for those who do not know her much) is from Elkhart, Indiana. She was raised in a huge Polish family (12 brothers and sisters) along with a lot of foster babies and other needy people in and out of the house. She presently has 70+ nieces and nephews. She has lived a very unique life. Upon graduating from Notre Dame in 1999, she spent almost 20 years in the missions serving the poor (including orphanages) as well as praying as a consecrated hermit all over the world–Siberia, Nigeria, Tanzania, South Africa, Philippines, Mexico, the Holy Land and all over Europe as well. Although she spent a lot of time away in silence praying, she loves children and is very fun and outgoing when it comes to serving young adults, as well as the little ones. She also spent her time in the missions giving retreats, doing simple catechesis, leading prayer groups, giving spiritual direction, helping in deliverance, changing diapers, feeding babies, and cleaning floors. After spending intense time serving in a mission, she would withdraw for periods of 'retreat' as a hermit (including three years as an official diocesan hermit with vows under a Bishop). The last few years she has spent as a full time nanny to infant triplets, twins, and several large families. She speaks many languages (poorly) and enjoys playing guitar, painting icons, baking, gardening, reading, writing, and simply filling in where there is the greatest need in the Church.

I have translated her six books. These books are *The Holiness of Womanhood, Out of the Darkness, In our Lady's Shadow: The Spirituality of Praying for Priests, A Heart Frozen in the Wilderness: The Reflection of a Siberian Missionary, Mornings with Mary (A Rosary Prayer book)* and *Raising Children of the Cross (Spiritual Formation of Children).*

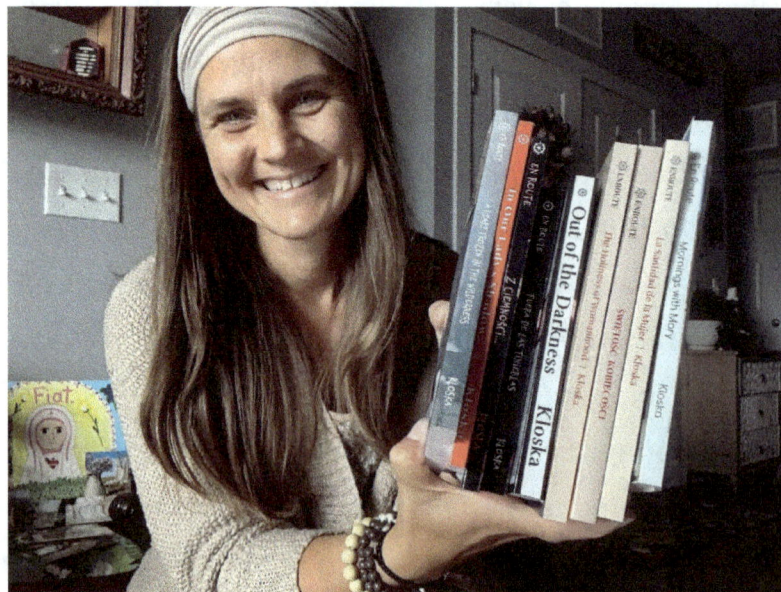

This huge work done in such a short time is a sign of God's presence in this task. This is not possible without God's will and Our Lady's favor. Her books left me with tears of sorrow and joy.

This life-giving and light-giving story (witness) began when I started translating Mary's first book, entitled ***The Holiness of Womanhood.*** When I started reading *The Holiness of Womanhood*, I was deeply touched with every word. This book introduced me to the high level of dignity of a woman. I read many times in the book of Genesis that God created women in his own image and likeness, and this book helped me to understand that image. I live in a country where in many families boys are given preference over girls. Of course, this does not happen in all families, but still it is a fact that the celebration of a new born baby boy is different and better. So, in this situation, girls from the very beginning seek to

deny their identity because they are not accepted. I have known many families that have many daughters, and still they want to have more children because they want a boy.

So, reading and translating this book *The Holiness of Womanhood* in this system of families left me with both tears of sorrow and joy. I read this book many times, and I prayed a lot while translating this book. I felt that God had answered my prayers. I have a daughter named Eliana; I love her very much. This book helped me to see God's image and likeness in my daughter.

Then I decided to take this book to other communities, churches, groups, and, of course, families to help them to have a better understanding of the holiness of womanhood. I felt that it is my responsibility given by God to bring this book to others. So, I completed the translation quickly. Printing this book was a challenge as well. But God provided what was needed to get it printed here in Pakistan.

As I shared earlier that teaching is my passion, so I prayed, and God gave me the opportunity to bring the message of this book to the people. I started with a small group. And I found girls and their mothers crying with joy. They expressed that this is the first time they are listening to these things.

I have shared a few pictures of these seminars, workshops, and conversations. In each session, people (both men and women) were happy to listen about the dignity of a woman. I still remember that in one of my seminars, a young girl came to me, and she was literally crying. I was a little confused. After some time, she told me that she always wanted to be a boy because no one was accepting her as a girl in the family. Parents wanted to have a son.

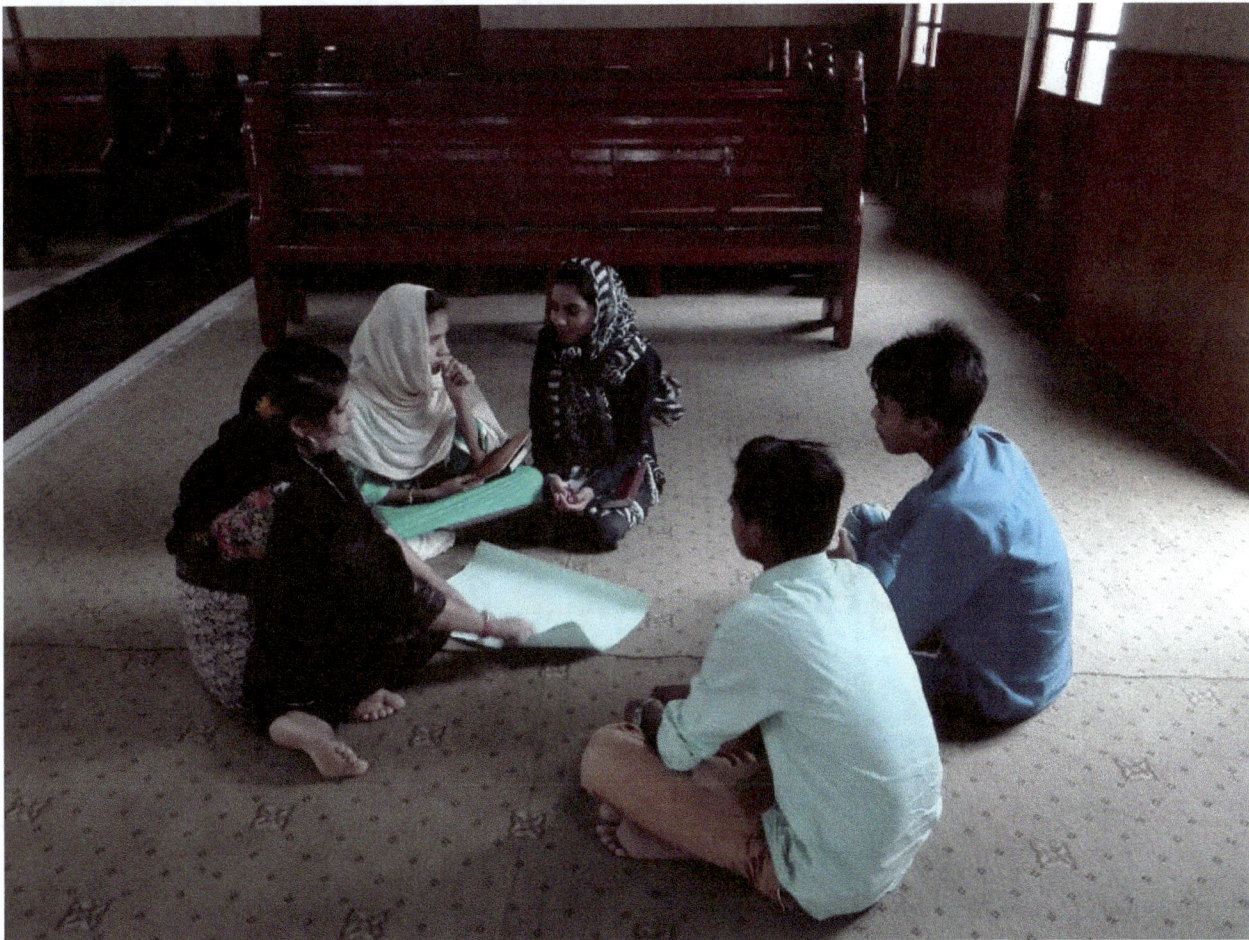

So, she shared that even she herself was not happy with her female identity. But she said that after listening to this book *The Holiness of Womanhood* about the dignity and value of a woman, she is happy that God created her as a girl.

This was a witness that God was working through these seminars. This book started changing the lives of many people. Even in one of my workshops, a man came to me and said that he has seven daughters. He wanted a boy. But after the talk, he shared that he is happy with his daughters. He also promised to respect his daughters and wife.

These stories of success always gave me joy and encouragement to do more. Many people, especially women, wanted to have this book. But the majority of our people are poor. They could not afford this book. So, I talked with Mary Kloska (the author), and she was happy to distribute this book free of cost.

I was busy distributing this book and doing awareness seminars when the second book of Mary Kloska was ready for printing. The title of the book was *Out of the Darkness*. Mary asked me to translate this book as well. Since I had seen the fruit of the first book, I decided to make the translation.

Once again, I was touched by Mary's depth of thought. *Out of the Darkness* is about the passion of Christ, about his love and sacrifice. Mary's book tells us about the power of Jesus'

cross. This is about persecution and love. This book had a significant reason to touch me and many Christians here in Pakistan. I live in a country where Christians are being persecuted because of their faith. We live in a minority here. Every day, there are cases of young girls being raped and being murdered. People are ignored because they are Christians. I will share few shocking incidents later in this book where people are murdered only because of their faith. So, this book met the exact need for me and my people.

Therefore, soon after translation we printed *Out of the Darkness* here in Pakistan. Once again, I targeted different groups, but with this book I approached a place where people were living in pain. This book gave some comfort to people in their persecution. I still remember in one of my sharing sessions with a group of women, a lady shared that her husband and son had been accused of false blasphemy and are in jail. Every day she was crying. In another group sharing, a lady shared that her son was murdered because of his faith.

I could not help that lady to bring her husband and son out of the prison. But believe me the passages and sharing from *Out of the Darkness* helped her to have some peace. These ladies shared that the suffering of Jesus and His divine love have consoled them. I was happy and surprised to see a smile on their faces.

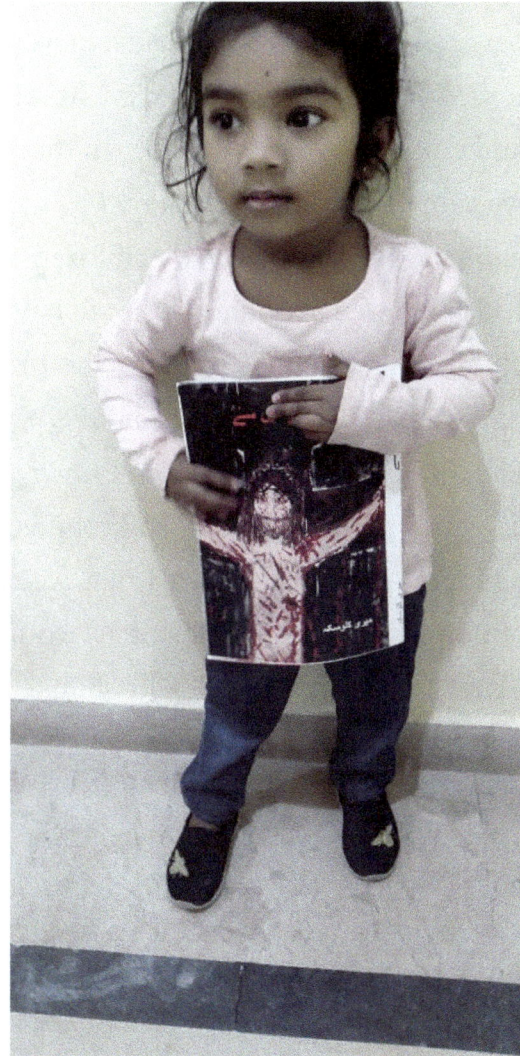

How did "Children of the Cross" come into being?

As I shared earlier that every day people are being persecuted here in Pakistan, young girls are forced to convert from their Christian religion, and children are being raped. In these situations, we cannot do much but pray. I was just thinking about a prayer group for children when Mary Kloska shared about her desire to have a group of children who would pray for the priests. Those days she was writing her book *In Our Lady's Shadow: The Spirituality of Praying for Priests*. This was a beautiful idea, so keeping my country situation in mind, I shared that we should have children's prayer groups that would pray for priests and persecuted Christians here in my place and all over the world.

Initially, the idea was to have children groups that would pray on the first Friday of the month. But in my situation, people, even small children, are spiritually hungry and thirsty. So, they started praying every day. They are praying every Friday and in a few places every day for priests and persecuted Christians. These children have power in their innocent and pure prayers. I have experienced that their prayers have changed situations and hearts. I never really thought that this translation work would turn into a ministry of "Children of the Cross." So now in Pakistan, these children are faithfully praying for priests, persecuted Christians, the sick, and for all those who are in need of our prayers. These groups are also praying the Rosary every day for those who are in need of Our Lady.

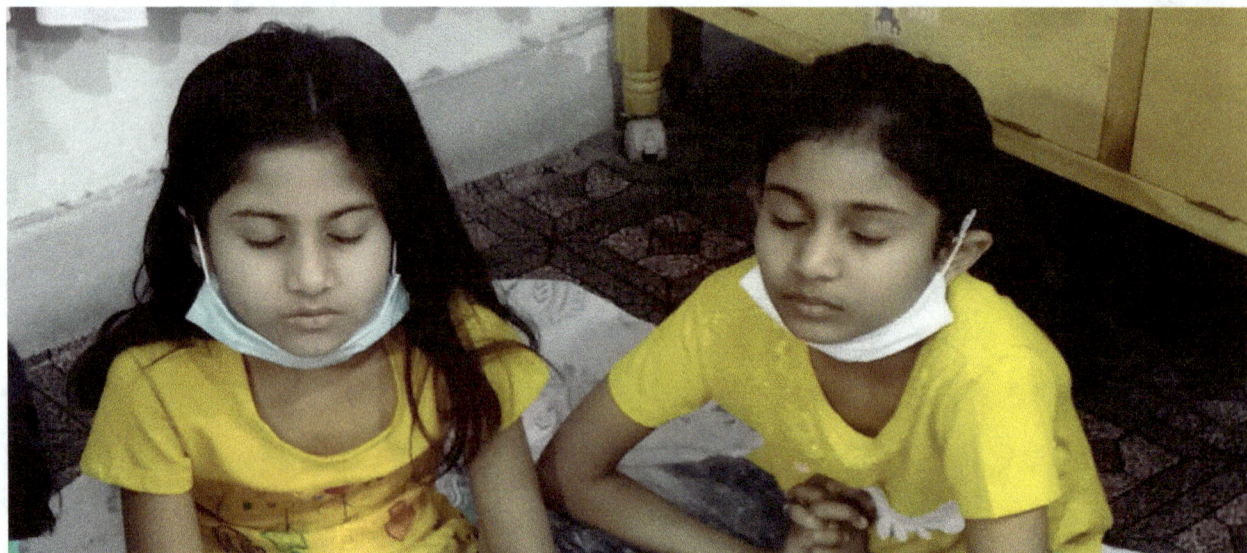

These children are very near to God. I am really happy and surprised to see that in these groups are children from other religions. I never expected that Muslim children would join our Rosary groups. These non-Christian children are coming for prayer with the permission of their parents. This is a miracle for my place. A place where Christians are being persecuted by Muslims, in the same place their children have started joining us for prayer.

The power of the Rosary is really something amazing. In Pakistan, Christians but Non-Catholics have different opinions about our Mother Mary. But now with these groups this gap is shrinking. People (children, men, and women) from various Christian denominations are happily joining us in our prayers.

Wherever persecution takes place, these children and their teachers are always ready to go and pray there. One morning, I got sad news that two small girls, Sozaina and Ena, ages six and eight years old, are being raped by a Muslim adult. And Muslims are trying to hide this issue by putting pressure on the families. This news really broke my and everyone's hearts. Young babies were being raped. Tears were everywhere. Then a few teachers and even small children for "Children of the Cross" decided to pray and go to their houses. This was a loving and sacred gesture from these children.

Little Ena with her father

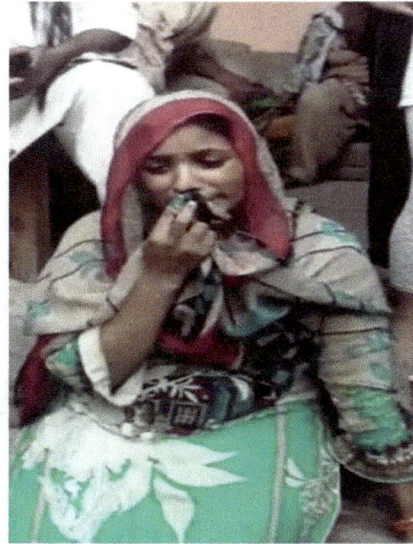

Ena's Mother

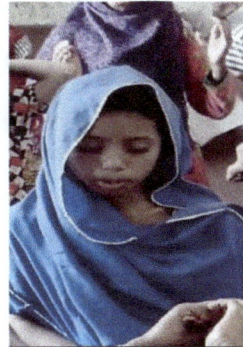

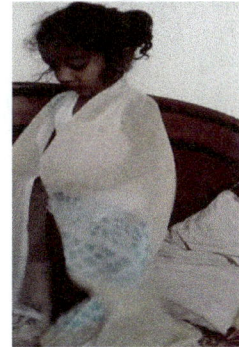

Special prayers for Sozaina and Ena were said by Children of the Cross in different places. These prayers were said for the comfort, peace and hope for these families.

Chapter 3
Mission in Pakistan and Afghanistan

This ministry of "Children of the Cross" was growing in number and spirituality when the fourth book of Mary Kloska came on the scene. The title of the book was *A Heart Frozen in the Wilderness: The Reflection of a Siberian Missionary*. In this book, Mary shares her experience as a Siberian Missionary. This is a deep book, filled with the kind of wisdom only a missionary comes to understand. She encountered God in different tough situations and people. Every missionary must read this book. This book is not only for missionaries but also for those who are willing to be. I have experienced in Pakistan that this book has awakened the zeal, flame, and love of mission among people.

I could read *A Heart Frozen in the Wilderness* again and again. This book has awakened the missionary spirit in me. I have used the stories from this book for my reflections. "Children of the Cross" groups are growing in numbers. One day, a pastor called me and asked me to start a

prayer group (Children of the Cross) in his place. I went there. Children asked me to tell them stories from the Bible, and I also shared many stories from Mary's book. Children were really inspired.

I translated this book and had a few launching ceremonies in different places. People were always happy to listen to this book. These stories (real experiences) always gave moral lessons to the listeners.

After reading this book, many people came to me and asked for a mission. Here I would like to mention that this book also changed the meaning of mission for my people. Our people always thought that when we do missions in other countries, a person leaves his or her country and goes to another to do a mission.

When these people were coming to me and asking for a mission, I was really stuck on how to help them. Since they were full of zeal to do something. This book really touched their missionary heart. So, we decided to start this mission in Pakistan.

(i) Mission in Sindh

Sindh is one of the provinces of Pakistan, located in the southeastern region of the country. Sindh is the third largest province of Pakistan by total area and second largest by population after Punjab. In Sindh, there are few villages that have totally unique and rich culture. They are different from Punjab. Their dresses, prayers, and language are different from Punjab. They are very hospitable. There are different communities in this place. A few pictures from this culture might give you a better understanding.

Since when I was with Franciscans, I did my pastoral work in this place and I know about their different and beautiful rituals. So, I decided that I would love to send people to Sindh for a mission. This was a new and unique idea. This was a kind of mission exchange.

Special study sessions and prayers sessions were held for the preparation of this mission work. Two devoted persons (a man and a woman) were accepted for this mission. One of the missionaries named Joshua, was (pictured on page 39) was a totally changed person after he got back. He is now assisting me in my ministry. He said that this mission experience has changed him and touched his heart. We wish and pray to continue this mission at least in Pakistan.

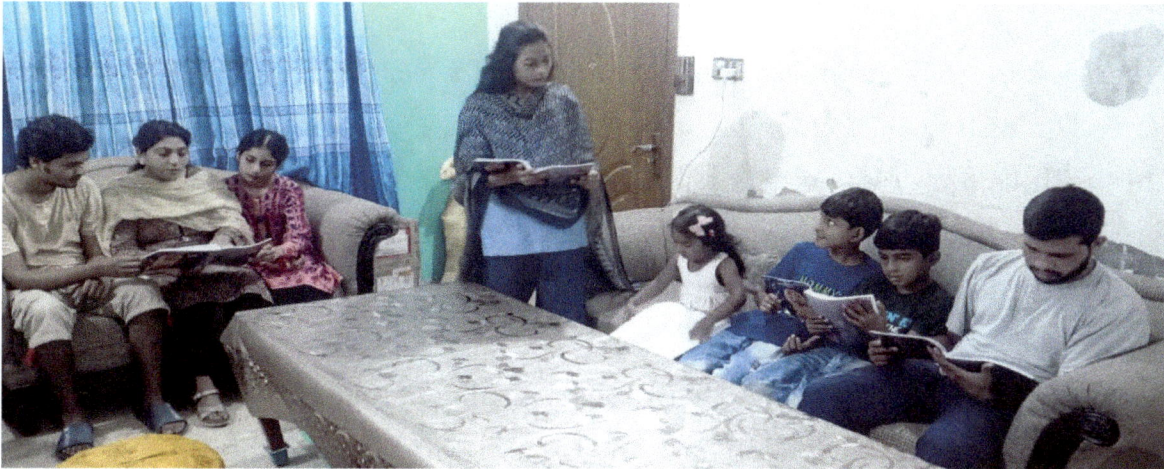

(ii) Mission in Afghanistan

The mission in Afghanistan is a complete miracle. I never thought that the "Children of the Cross" ministry would enter Afghanistan. Actually, I was thinking with my human mind, but with God everything is possible. The growth and impact of "Children of the Cross" are incredible. God has been visibly with us. I always prayed to Our Lady for the conversion of Pakistan, but she was preparing and planning for the conversion of Afghanistan.

The mission in Afghanistan started with a short email sent to me by Dr. Sebastian Mahfood, OP. I still remember this was 18th of August 2021, when I got a short message from him,

"Good afternoon, Aqif, It may be important to get this book to Afghanistan in light of the Taliban takeover. Know anyone who can translate it into Dari?"

I immediately started searching for people who could translate into Dari (Dari is an official language of Afghanistan). Since I knew few people who could translate, I chose one person. And this was my response:

Greetings!
After two days' hard work, I would like to update about our project in Afghanistan.
I have talked to a person from Afghanistan (as I shared with you already, this community has been living here in Pakistan since long). He is ready to help us translate. He

is a good, educated person. He is a Muslim man but very nice. His name is Muhamad Mustafa. One of his brothers and sister have been murdered by Taliban in Afghanistan.

So, this remaining family came here. He is willing to help us because he himself has gone through suffering because of the Taliban. The Afghan community in Pakistan shared with me that these books will be a blessing for persecuted people there. The persecution they are experiencing there is really unbearable. I personally see hope and light through these books as I have experienced in Pakistan. This community further shared that it is really urgent to console people there.

This was a risky task, but God was with us. There was a team who worked on this project. Translations, typing, proof reading—everything was happening in a small room. "Children of the Cross" in Pakistan and many others were continually praying for this project. I always believed that this project was from God, so though I faced many difficulties and threats, I knew these books would reach there. We chose *The Holiness of Womanhood* and *Out of the Darkness* for Dari translation.

Sending books to Afghanistan was also not an easy task. The person who volunteered to go along shared that it was a risky job. I received a message from him. He shared that in many places there were problems, but God saved him and books miraculously.

This is a witness that God saved him in many places. On many occasions, he felt that he would lose the books and even his life. But our lady was there to protect him and the books. He shared that in more than ten places he felt threatened, and he really felt he would die now. He told me that he kept saying rosaries for five continuous days.

Greetings, I have just got a short but detailed note from Afghanistan:

Dear brother!

God be praised.

First of all, greetings from a Catholic family that I am staying with. This family has read Mary Kloska's both books (*The Holiness of Womanhood* and *Out of the Darkness*). This family (husband and wife, two children and three friends that keep visiting them) is entirely thankful for these books. The wife is a nurse, and she has brought this book to other nurses in the hospital. She has done this work secretly. Because if someone from the hospital management comes to know about this she will be fired out. She is reading this book with other nurses secretly, and she said that among these nurses there are Muslim nurses as well. She witnessed that all the nurses who are reading this book cry with sorrow and happiness. One of the Muslim nurses from the group said that the teaching in this book is the true teaching. This is real life. We are dying every day, every second. These books have given us light.

The husband has given these books to a few teachers and those whom he meets in the market. We are doing this all very silently and secretly. A hidden church is taking shape. We cannot meet regularly because most of the time our activities are being watched. I shared with them about your group 'Children of the Cross'. So, the children from this family, their three friend's children, and a few nurses' children meet secretly just to say a short prayer.

Please convey a message to Sister Mary Kloska that her books are seeds of peace in this barren land. Here Taliban are always ready to kill others, but her books are giving the message of hope. Please tell Sister Mary that one day her books will convert people here though a very very long way to travel. But we have started travelling this path with her books.

This Catholic family with other friends and people are planning to focus on children so that the next generation will bring peace. Because it is very hard to preach to the adults here. It is so dangerous. But we are sharing these books with adults as well where we feel secure.

Please tell Sister Mary that the hidden church has started. This certain hidden church and other places where people pray secretly are always in danger. Only prayer can convert people. Praise the lord for the first time Children of the Cross is here in Afghanistan. The first group of children of prayer have formed here, though a very small group, but it will grow. This Christmas they have distributed many books, and I hope their feedback will come soon. This Catholic family would love to write to Sister Mary Kloska, but they are afraid because their internet (emails, messengers, WhatsApp's) is always being monitored. And if someone knows that they are writing to someone in the USA, this can cause problems. But one day they will write.

I have seen their situation, so I feel sharing pictures of these activities is too early. This can bring them trouble. So, I am waiting for the right time. Please you and Sister Mary pray for me, too. I need your prayers. God bless you more, and God bless Sister Mary. These people are very grateful to Sister Mary. A few people here say that she is not Sister Mary but Mother Mary for them.

(iii) Testimonies from Persecuted Christians

(How Mary Kloska's books have strengthened, healed, and helped them.)

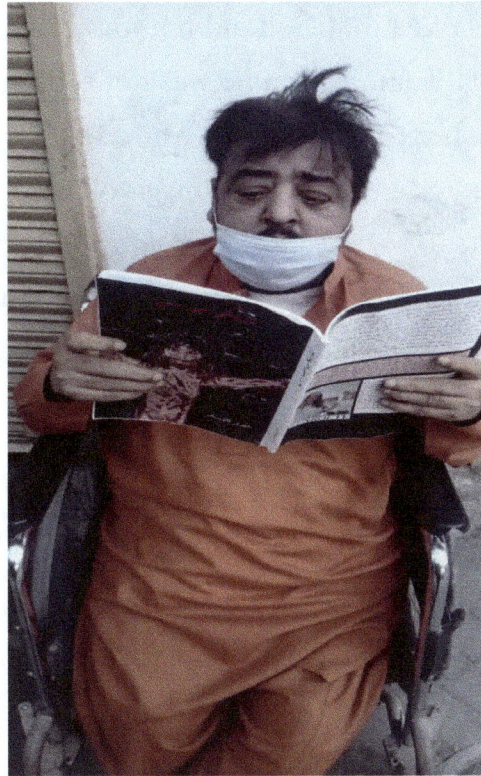

Mr. Shahid Khan

Here is Mr. Shahid, a friend of mine. He died at the age of about 46. For most of his life, he lived in a wheelchair. Since he did not have opportunities to learn, he always had wrong ways of earning money. He was always suffering. He did not accept his condition.

The pain he went through was too much. I gave him the Urdu translation of *Out of the Darkness*. He read this book, and eventually he converted to Christianity. He left all his wrong ways. Ultimately, he accepted his pain and suffering. He accepted that God loved him. Earlier, he always complained that God did not love him.

One day, I got a call from his family that he was not feeling well. I was really surprised that when I reached his house he requested me to read a few passages from *Out of the Darkness*. He admitted that he wanted to hear from this book before he left this earth. I read a few passages to him with tears in my eyes. I shared with him about our project in Afghanistan. And he admitted that these books are important because they give life and hope. When later I came back, I learned he had fallen asleep in the Lord.

I thanked God for his life. I am really thankful to God that Mary Kloska's books not only give life to people on their earthly journey but also help them to prepare and make their heavenly journey. This incident assured us that our project in Afghanistan is really important and urgent.

Joshua Edwin

This is Joshua Edwin, a faithful and God fearing person. He is inspired when he reads these books, and now he is inspiring others. He is the one who committed himself to go on mission in Sindh. He promised to read this book to different groups of women who cannot read.

My name is Joshua Edwin. I am 26 years old. I kept waiting for this Urdu book since long. When I read it I really felt my connection with my mother. I have experienced being born again. I was always wondering something is missing in my life. After reading this book I knew what was missing.

Every day I was listening to news of young girls being raped, being forced to conversion. I was really sad. This book gave me hope and I am going to bring this hope to other hopeless families.

I thank you from the bottom of my heart to the writer of this book and of course the translator of this book. I have decided that I will be sharing this book's message to at least more than hundred women who cannot read. There are many poor women who want to read it but cannot afford. I promise I will buy few for them.

This book gave me peace and hope as a man, so how much it will give to women.

Thank you Lord, thank you Mary (the writer) and many many thanks to translator who have made it possible for those who cannot understand English.

Michelle

Hello, I am Michelle from Pakistan. I am a medical student. I always wanted to read something which could give depth to my womanhood. Thanks God my prayers are answered as I got a book in Urdu. I have met many young girls in my University who are looking for some peace, hope and meaning of life.

As a young girl, I was sad to hear many girls who said, we wish we would be a boy. Why? Because as women they are not treated well. But this book give me hope to bring hope to them. I read this book and today I contacted the translator again and shared my story with him.

I was able to share this book with two other young girls. They kept crying. I asked them but they could not give any answer. It is only today they were able to tell me that, this book helped them to say thank you to Lord being creating them as women.

Thank you to the writer, who has brought us to the point that women are image of God. Bundle of thanks to translator who made it possible that every can read it.

Thank you God for this holy book.

Suleman Vincent

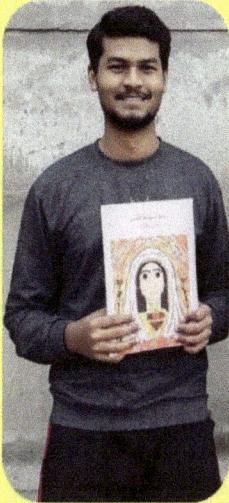

My name is Suleman Vincent. I am a student of Fsc. I am very active in youth and church activities. Once I was studying the book of Genesis in the church. And the leader said that men and women are created on the image of God. He also tried to explain this concept, which truly could not understand.

But when I read this book, I was able to understand that women are really created on the image of God. Yesterday I went back to that pastor and said that today I understood the meaning of image of God in women. I gave him this book to read. I also encouraged my class fellows in the church to read this book especially young girls.

And this morning, after church service, my pastor bought 10 books for poor women who wanted to read but could not afford. Thank you very much pastor.

Thank you very much Sister Mary for this beautiful book. And thank you to Sir Aqif Shahzad who translated it and made it possible that I could understand it very well.

(iv) A Few Emails that describe the miracles that these books have performed

On Mother's Day (May 9, 2021)

This is so beautiful to hear... (even if sad)...

What a beautiful Mother's Day gift to hear that God is using my little nothing book to touch and heal not only Catholics and Muslims, but Christians of other denominations.

All I can do is thank my Urdu translator in Pakistan_for doing such an incredible job gardening and watering the seed of my books in the hearts of his people... Read this testimony below!!!

Come Holy Spirit!

"Greetings and wish you a very happy Mother Day,

Three days ago, I got a call from one pastor (he doesn't belong to a Catholic church—he's some other denomination) who invited me to conduct a short session for a Mother's Day program. I said that I would do it happily, and I asked him the purpose of this program.

The pastor said that he has a group of young women in his church. And in this group two women were raped about one year back. Then there is a woman whose husband has been in prison because he was falsely accused of blaspheme. He has been in jail for more than four years.

Then next I was surprised to listen to him. He asked that I please share with my group from the book *The Holiness of Womanhood*. I asked him how he knew about this book.

Then I came to know that about a few months back this pastor was attending a prayer service in some other church. And there he heard the witness of three women who got hope, peace, comfort, and some kind of conversion after reading this book. So, he took my contact number from those women and called me.

Then I said yes and requested that he should also invite men. Because men must also listen to this all. I believe that in Pakistan many women are being deprived of their rights and dignity because of men.

So, I went there and I shared chapter 2 "Woman as Gift" and chapter 4 "Woman as Mother." Then at the end, I asked them to reflect about the questions that are given at the end chapter 2.

"What are my gifts of my body that God gave to me? How is my body a gift?"

Believe me those women who were raped had tears in their eyes. I asked them to write their feelings to God, their charts (I gave them charts to write) were wet. Even men had tears in their eyes when they listened to them.

At the end of the program, I saw a smile on those women and some hope. I promised them that I would give them some books very soon.

(Here are a) few pictures of this program.

Thank you, Jesus, thank you Mother Mary and really thank you Mary Kloska.

We always knew that suffering is bad and curse but after reading your books we know suffering is also a gift of God, suffering is also a sign of love."

May 31, 2021

"Greetings of the Lord and Mother Mary be with you!

Indeed, I had a very busy weekend. I really praise the Lord for all he is doing. I was able to say the rosary with the Children of the Cross. I asked them to bring pictures for all the persecuted people. You can see in one of the pictures that they have really brought so many pictures that we have to choose a few. But this showed their faith in prayer.

In one picture, a lady is leading in prayer. She prayed for all the people especially who are tortured because they are Christians.

In another of the pictures, a man is leading in a prayer. He is also leading Children of the Cross. These poor children are very happy when they pray.

In one of the places that I visited yesterday, I told children that we should pray for all the poor and persecuted. So, one of the children from the group said that we are also in the same condition. I told her, "Then lets pray for ourselves as well."

I showed a short movie to one group about Mother Mary. And then I also showed a small documentary about persecution of Christian people in my country.

Then the good thing is that, I was able to meet a group of Muslim leaders. They were all from big institutions and have their say. I shared your book with them. I also told them about facts and figures about what is happening in Pakistan. I told them that each year 1,000 Pakistani girls are forcibly converted to Islam. Honestly speaking, it is very dangerous to tell these things, but I feel someone has to take steps. They listened to me. One of the Muslim leaders was a professor in an Islamic University. He said he would like to keep this book in the university library. I gave him a copy of *The Holiness of Womanhood*.

That is really true that every year more than a thousand girls are converted to Islam forcefully.

Then a sad incident happened a few days back. In the hospital, one early morning, a Christian nurse was raped by three Muslims. A really sad incident. It is true that in my place Christians are not safe, especially women. I am trying to reach that nurse just to tell her that we are praying for her.

Your books have given me courage to do something for my people in Pakistan. Your books are a source of hope and peace. Your books have given a purpose in my life to serve my community. My people have found peace in your writings. This is God's will, His call for me to be the voice of my people.

Thank you very much and I need your continued prayers."

June 6, 2021

"Greetings and Happy Sunday,

I just got back from church. Today once again I was invited to a church to preach *The Holiness of Womanhood*. It was a deep experience. There were about 45 participants. I think only 10 were men, and the rest were all young women. I am sharing a few pictures of this activity.

I gave them a brief introduction of the book, and then I read a few chosen texts from the book. All the young (girls) were full of joy and wonder while listening to the book. There were a few mothers as well. I could see their eyes with tears of happiness and gratitude.

Then I divided them into groups. Group work is always amazing because in small groups people feel that it is easy to share their true feelings. I asked them to write and share what they were feeling before they listened to this book and what they are feeling after having listened to this book. Their response touched me.

What they were feeling before they listened to this book:

- Women are not born in the image of God.
- God loves men more than women.
- Women have nothing to do in the plan of salvation.

What they felt after they listened to this book:

- God has created them on HIS own image.
- God loves us very much.
- We are helpers of God.
- A woman (Mother Mary) gave birth to Jesus, so all women are Holy and can share Jesus with others.
- Women played and still play a vital role in salvation.

At the end many of the participants came to me and asked to learn more about the author (Mary Kloska). Thousands of prayers were offered for the writer of this book.

In our culture, we mostly keep the Bible in a separate fixed place. Women came and said they would keep this book close to the Bible as this book is also life touching and changing.

I also shared with the group about "Children of the Cross". All of them promised to pray on Friday for persecuted Christians and all priests. A few (married women) promised to send their children for Rosary.

Mary, once again, thank you very much for enriching our culture with this spirituality. We did not know what to do, but your books have prepared a way for us. Thanks for being Hope in our hopelessness.

Thank you very much Dr. Sebastian for always being available to us. Thank you for always listening to us. And thanks for your encouragement.

Blessings!"

June 8, 2021

"Greetings in the name of our Lord!

Mostly, I visit communities on weekends. But sometimes if I feel that I am needed I cannot refuse. The same thing happened today. I got a call from a rural community. This place is located far from Lahore (my place); indeed, this is a persecuted community. Poverty is beyond our imagination. Still many people here can read and write.

Today, I was asked to share the book *Out of the Darkness*. As you can see in the pictures I was welcomed warmly. I was surprised to see the number of people, almost seventy of them. And only six were men. So, when I saw such a great number of women, I also shared *The Holiness of Womanhood*.

In this place every house has terrible stories. They do not have enough to eat, and they do not have equal rights (even not basic human rights). Being Christians, they are deprived of rights. A few can read and write; still they are offered only low jobs. Many of the women work in big houses, and there they are physically and psychologically tortured every day. They cannot even complain.

I spent a couple of hours with these women, young, old, and even children. The whole group including me had the Holy Spirit experience.

Since many of them could not read, I had to read aloud for them. I also invited young women who could read to lead.

At the end *Out of the Darkness* and *The Holiness of Womanhood*, they were able to turn their tears into joy, their hopelessness into hope, and their uncertainty into peace. At the very end, a group of young children did a cultural dance to say thank you to God for their life. Before this talk, this group could not imagine dancing. They were really sad and felt dark. After this, they felt the experience of coming out of the darkness.

At the end, one decade of the Rosary was recited for Mary Kloska for reason of her love for our people. I also mentioned *In Our Lady's Shadow*, and I promised that next time I would read that book to them.

Now it is 12:50 a.m. I wanted to write to you tomorrow in the morning, but one woman said please just go home and say thank you to Mary Kloska. So, I promised them.

Blessings to you Mary, and once again thank you God who chose you for our people.

THANK YOU VERY MUCH FROM ME AND FROM TODAY'S GATHERING OF WOMEN."

June 19, 2021

"Greetings to you in the name of our Lord!

Here are a few pictures of this Friday and Saturday activities. On Friday evening, I went to a place where once again the majority of the people are being persecuted in one or another way. People, especially children and women, are physically and spiritually hungry. They are living in a certain fear. They really do not know what prayer is and the importance of prayer. They do not pray for themselves, so how can we imagine that they pray for others.

So, I went there with *In Our Lady's Shadow: The Spirituality of Praying for Priests*.

And it was good that one of my friends who is a priest also attended this session. The priest kept his promise. He promised that he would join whenever he has time.

The pictures that I am sharing of this community are not very clear. They don't have proper light in the church. Later, I reflected that they do not have light in their lives as well.

I shared a few texts with them from this book. I am feeling some peace that at the end they were willing to pray for others and themselves. I asked them about the hardships and persecution of their lives. They came with so many things with tears in their eyes. Their stories also brought tears to my eyes. But God turned these tears into joy at the end.

Then our group "Children of the Cross" made a special prayer for persecuted priests and Christians. I asked them to draw what they are feeling. In their paintings, fear and uncertainty was clear. This group is very active and good in prayer. So, I have planned to bring this group (their parents have given me permission) to other places. This will help me to encourage others.

I am very delighted and humbled to share with you that since I am translating your book *A Heart Frozen in the Wilderness*, I shared my experience with this group. So, this little group of children themselves asked me to pray for the conversion of Russia.

I never thought that in Pakistan, in my little town and in my house and in my other poor churches, we would pray for Russia. When children and parents were sharing about their hardships, I added a few stories from *A Heart Frozen*. People in both places said that the suffering of Russia and Pakistan are similar somehow.

Then at the end we had a heart-touching prayer.

God bless you, Mary. I need your continued prayers as your books have proven a mustard seed in the hearts of my poor, simple, innocent, and persecuted people.

I need your prayer because it's a long way, and I am ready to travel this with people and for people.

Blessings!"

July 2, 2021

"Greetings in the name of our Lord!

I thank God that my last weekend has been full of blessings. I really experienced the love of Jesus among wounded people. I was able to reach different communities and churches. A few places were quite good, but a few were really poor and dirty. Yet in both conditions, the love of God was visible. The Holy Spirit was with me and with all whom I met.

There was a man about forty years old. He never came to church. I met him a few weeks back and invited him to come. So, he came to attend. He said he was shy to come to church as he always felt that his sins were stopping him from receiving God's love. At the end of our program, he prayed with tears. You can see in one picture this man kneeling down. He said I did not know how to pray. But he experienced that some lady (of course, I believe it was our Lady) was guiding him to pray. He said during reflection from the book *In Our Lady's Shadow: The Spirituality of Praying for Priests,* he got the courage to pray. He kept praying for a long time.

Then, I also visited small children who have basic needs at home but rarely experience God's love. I sat with them. Prayed with them. When I was sitting with them, I was using references from the book *A Heart Frozen in the Wilderness.* They felt this kind of love for the first time.

Then in one church during group work (you can see in one picture), young women and men had deep spiritual conversation with me.

Here one miracle happened. As I was sharing a few thoughts about the condition of Russia (I am translating *A Heart Frozen in the Wilderness,* so this book is always in my mind and heart), one lady who was about 48 years old (she never got married), said that she would like to adopt a spiritual son or daughter. She said after listening to me she feels it is her responsibility that she must bring one or two children to God.

Thank you very much, Mary Kloska, for your spiritual wisdom. Our Lady is really showering Her blessings through your books. Many groups who are not Catholic now feel easy to talk about Mother Mary (though these groups are still in small numbers, but earlier they did not exist at all).

Again, sincere thanks for your book *A Heart Frozen in the Wilderness*. It is every day giving my life direction and reminding me to pray for all missionaries.

Blessings to you all!"

July 18, 2021

From PAKISTAN:

"A sad incident happened a few days back. Eight years old Suzaina Shahzad (Christian school girl) has been raped. I know this place very well. I have followed this news on social media only. I will go tomorrow to investigate it properly. But the news is sad and true.

We had special prayers for this girl. We are also asking you to pray for her. I will share more about his news after I visit personally.

In this tough and darkness, Our Lady is always there to be with us.

July 19, 2021

Greetings!

I am sorry for the late reply.

Yes Mary, I went to Soziana's house. It was indeed very painful to see her and her family. She is about eight years old and studies in class three. She is a Christian girl. A Muslim person has raped her. The school is trying to hide this matter and protect this man. Many times, these kinds of incidents take place here in my region.

When I went there for the first time, I really found it hard to give her hope. I talked to her mother, but they were so hopeless.

Then I came back and prayed a lot. I prayed many hours to Our Lady. I told Mother Mary that Soziana is her daughter and to please guide me to console her.

Then the next day I went again with four young ladies who have studied your books thoroughly and found peace and hope. I told these young women about this incident. They went along with me. We had a prayer session there, and everyone shared her experience with the mother and her little daughter.

All praise to God. Your books really gave this hopeless family a hope. They were in a dark situation and found light.

I spent a couple of hours giving a reflection from your book *Out of the Darkness*, chapter two. I shared from this chapter that Jesus also went through darkness and pain, and this pain helped him to be more close to God. I told mother and little baby that Jesus is with you in this pain. You are not alone. Mother Mary is bearing your pain.

I was amazed that after a couple of hours they felt peace (though they were still crying). It was a miracle. Then I also shared many experiences of yours from the book *A Heart Frozen in the Wilderness*. I told them that even in Russian there are countless parents and children living in pain and away from God. I told them how you experienced God in this dark life in Russia. I tried to tell them how God is present in our pains.

There is no doubt that they are still in pain, looking for justice. No one is supporting them. Everyone is protecting that wicked person who raped. But after I visited these young women with your books, they experienced peace, light, and some hope.

Thank you very much, Mary. Your books are giving hope and light. Thanks for your continued prayers. I told them that you (Mary Kloska) are regularly praying for them. They acknowledged that they felt the presence of the Holy Spirit praying with them while reading your books.

This family acknowledged that your books have helped them like scripture. I will visit this family again soon.

I am thankful to these young women who helped me, and these women are thankful to you as your books are helping them.

I have attached the pictures of young women and that little girl with her parents.

Thank you, Mary."

Chapter 4

Christianity and Persecuted Christians in Pakistan

Christianity and persecution in Pakistan go together. This is a bitter reality that every day Christians in Pakistan suffer in different ways. This suffering can be of any type, such as depriving Christians of their rights, discrimination, injustice, torture, death. Life is uncertain for Christians in Pakistan. Even those Christians who are living in a safe environment can be caught any time. Every day, sad and shocking incidents take place. Before I share my brief reflection about this brutal persecution, I would like to share few information about Christianity, adapted from Wikipedia, the free encyclopedia:

According to the 2017 Census, the proportion of Christians in Pakistan was estimated at about 1.27% of the population. Of these, approximately half are Catholic and half Protestant. A small number of Eastern Orthodox Christians and Oriental Orthodox Christians also live in Pakistan.

Pakistan's Christian community developed a "growing sense of concern," particularly over the strict blasphemy laws–which restrict any insults against the Islamic prophet Muhammad and makes the crime punishable by death–which many activists viewed as "being abused to target religious minorities. In the 1990s, some Christians were arrested on charges of blasphemy, and for protesting that appeared to insult Islam. John Joseph, a bishop in Faisalabad, committed suicide to protest the execution of a Christian man on blasphemy charges.

In 2009, a series of attacks killed eight Christians in Gojra, including four women and a child. In 2013, a suicide bombing at a Church in Peshawar left more than 100 people dead, and a series of attacks at churches in Lahore in 2015 left 14 dead. On March 27, 2016, over seventy people were killed when a suicide bomber targeting Christians celebrating Easter (though the majority of victims were Muslim in this instance) attacked a playground in Lahore.

Persecution

After the partition of India and the formation of Pakistan in 1947, many Sikhs were forced to migrate to an independent India. Many Christians worked under Sikh landlords, and when they departed the western parts of the Punjab region, the Government of Pakistan appropriated Sikh property to Muslims arriving from East Punjab. This caused over 300,000 Christians in Pakistan to become homeless. On top of that, rogue Muslims threatened Christians that Pakistan was made for Muslims only and that if Christians wanted to stay there, they had to live a life of servitude and perform sanitation work. Some Christians were therefore murdered for refusing to pick up garbage. In 1951, seventy-two Muslims were charged with the murder of eleven Christians after communal riots over agricultural land erupted.

Many churches built during the colonial Indian period, prior to the partition, remain locked, with the Pakistani government refusing to hand them over to the Christian community. Others have been victims of church arsons or demolitions. In 1971, East Pakistan became independent as Bangladesh, and the majority of Pakistan's

Hindus, who lived in Bangladesh, were severed from Pakistan. Pakistan became a culturally monolithic, increasingly Islamic state, with smaller religious minorities than ever.

With the governments of Zulfikar Ali Bhutto and Zia ul-Haq, more stringently Islamic laws transformed Pakistan. Conversion to other faiths than Islam is not prohibited by law, but culture and social pressures do not favor such conversions. Muslims who change their faith to Christianity are subject to societal pressure. Extremely controversial were the blasphemy laws, which made it treacherous for non-Muslims to express themselves without being accused of being un-Islamic. Zia also introduced the Sharia as a basis for lawmaking, reinforced by Nawaz Sharif in 1991. Coerced conversions to Islam from Christianity are a major source of concern for Pakistani Christians, and the minority faces threats, harassment, and intimidation tactics from extremists.

Discrimination in the Constitution

Christians, along with other non-Muslim minorities, are discriminated against in the Constitution of Pakistan. Non-Muslims are barred from becoming President or Prime Minister. Furthermore, they are barred from being judges in the Federal Shariat Court, which has the power to strike down any law deemed un-Islamic. In 2019, Naveed Amir, a Christian member of the National Assembly moved a bill to amend the article 41 and 91 of the Constitution, which would allow non-Muslims to become Prime Minister and President of Pakistan. However, Pakistan's parliament blocked the bill.

In 2019, a Christian journalist quit the channel Dunya News after she was allegedly persecuted for her faith by co-workers and insulted for not converting to Islam.

Blasphemy Laws

Several hundred Christians, along with Muslims themselves (though much fewer in comparison), have been prosecuted under Pakistan's blasphemy laws, and death sentences have been handed out to at least a dozen.

Pakistani law mandates that any "blasphemies" of the Quran are to be met with punishment. On July 28, 1994, Amnesty International urged Pakistan's Prime Minister, Benazir Bhutto, to change the law because it was being used to terrorize religious minorities. She tried but was unsuccessful. However, she modified the laws to make them more moderate. Her changes were reversed by the Nawaz Sharif administration. Some people accused of blasphemy have been killed in prison or shot dead in court, and even if pardoned, may remain in danger from imams in their local village.

Ayub Masih, a Christian, was convicted of blasphemy and sentenced to death in 1998. He was accused by a neighbor of stating that he supported British writer Salman Rushdie, author of *The Satanic Verses*. Lower appeals courts upheld the conviction. However, before the Pakistan Supreme Court, his lawyer was able to prove that the accuser had used the conviction to force Masih's family off their land and then acquired control of the property. Masih has been released.

On September 22, 2006, a Pakistani Christian named Shahid Masih was arrested and jailed for allegedly violating Islamic "blasphemy laws" in the country of Pakistan. He is at present held in confinement and has expressed fear of reprisals by Islamic fundamentalists. (Note that the name "Masih", which comes from Arabic المسيحيين Al-Masihiyyin, "Christians," is a common surname in Pakistan and India among Christians.)

In November 2010, Asia Bibi was sentenced to death by hanging for "blasphemy"; the sentence would have had to have been upheld in a higher court before it could be executed. Bibi was acquitted in 2018.

In August 2012, Rimsha Masih, a Christian girl, reportedly 11 or 14 years old, and an illiterate with mental disabilities was accused of blasphemy for burning pages from a book containing Quranic verses. The allegation came from a Muslim cleric who himself has subsequently been accused by the police of framing the girl. The girl, and later the cleric, were both arrested and released on bail.

Forced conversions

In October 2020, the Pakistani High Court upheld the validity of a forced marriage between 44-year-old Ali Azhar and 13-year-old Christian Arzoo Raja. Raja was abducted by Azhar, forcibly wed to Azhar, and then forcibly converted to Islam by Azhar. Human rights organizations estimate that upwards of 1,000 Christian, Hindu, and Sikh girls are abducted each year. A large portion of them are then forced to convert to Islam.

Forced displacements

Since 2014, the Capital Development Authority (CDA), a public benefit corporation responsible for providing municipal services in Islamabad, has been targeting and demolishing illegal slums which are largely occupied by Christians in the city. The Supreme Court put on hold the demolitions and ordered from the CDA a written justification to it. The CDA replied that "Most of these katchi abadies [slums] are under the occupation of the Christian community. It seems this pace of occupation of land by the Christian community may increase. Removal of katchi abadies is very urgent to provide [a] better environment to the citizen[s] of Islamabad and to protect the beauty of Islamabad." Various human rights activists condemned the response.

On November 9, 2020, Yasmin Masih and her son Usman Masih, both Christians, were murdered in Ahmad Nagar Chattha by Hussain Shakoor, a Muslim.

In May 2021, Muslim nurses in the Mental Government Hospital in Lahore occupied the Christian hospital chapel and raised Islamic slogans. Christian nurses, who use the chapel daily for prayer, pleaded for their protection.

Muslim extremist violence against Christians

Christians in Pakistan report being targeted by Tehrik-i-Taliban Pakistan.

On 9 August 2002 gunmen threw grenades into a chapel on the grounds of the Taxila Christian Hospital in northern Punjab, 24 kilometres (15 miles) west of Islamabad, killing four, including two nurses and a paramedic, and wounding 25 men and women.

On September 25, 2002, unidentified Muslim gunmen shot dead six people at a Christian charity in Karachi's central business district. They entered the third-floor offices of the Institute for Peace and Justice (IPJ) and shot their victims in the head. All of the victims were Pakistani Christians. Karachi police chief Tariq Jamil said the victims had their hands tied, and their mouths had been covered with tape. On 25 December 2002, several days after an Islamic cleric called for Muslims to kill Christians, two burqa-clad Muslim gunmen tossed a grenade into a Presbyterian church during a Christian sermon in Chianwala in east Pakistan, killing three girls.

After the Karachi killings, Shahbaz Bhatti, the head of the All Pakistan Minority Alliance, told BBC News Online, "We have become increasingly victimised since the launch of the US-led international War on Terror. It is, therefore, the responsibility of the international community to ensure that the government protects us."

In November 2005, 3,000 militant Islamists attacked Christians in Sangla Hill in Pakistan and destroyed Roman Catholic, Salvation Army, and United Presbyterian churches. The attack was over allegations of violation of blasphemy laws by a Pakistani Christian named Yousaf Masih. The attacks were condemned by some political parties in Pakistan. However, Pakistani Christians have expressed disappointment that they have not received justice. Samson Dilawar, a parish priest in Sangla Hill, said the police have not committed to trial any of those arrested for committing the assaults, and the Pakistani government did not inform the Christian community that a judicial inquiry was underway by a local judge. He said that Muslim clerics still "make hateful speeches about Christians" and "continue insulting Christians and our faith."

In February 2006, churches and Christian schools were targeted in protests over publication of the Jyllands-Posten cartoons in Denmark, leaving two elderly women injured and many homes and much property destroyed. Some of the mobs were stopped by police, but not all. On June 5, 2006, a Pakistani Christian stonemason named Nasir Ashraf was working near Lahore when he drank water from a public facility using a glass chained to the facility. He was immediately assaulted by Muslims for "polluting the glass". A mob gathered and beat Ashraf, calling him a "Christian dog". Bystanders encouraged the beating, saying it was a "good" deed that would help the attackers get into heaven. Ashraf was hospitalized. In August 2006, a church and Christian homes were attacked in a village outside of Lahore in a land dispute. Three Christians were seriously injured and one reported missing after about 35 Muslims burned buildings, desecrated Bibles, and attacked Christians. Based, in part, on such incidents, Pakistan was recommended by the U.S. Commission on International Religious Freedom (USCIRF) in May 2006 to be designated as a "Country of Particular Concern" (CPC) by the Department of State.

In July 2008, a mob stormed a Protestant church during a prayer service on the outskirts of Pakistan's largest city, Karachi, denouncing the Christians as "infidels" and injuring several, including a pastor

The 2009 Gojra riots was a series of violent pogroms against Christian minorities by Muslims. In June 2009, International Christian Concern reported the rape and killing of a Christian man in Pakistan, for refusing to convert to Islam. In March 2011, Shahbaz Bhatti was killed by gunmen after he spoke out against Pakistan's blasphemy laws. The UK increased financial aid to the country, sparking criticism of British foreign secretary

William Hague. Cardinal Keith O'Brien stated, "To increase aid to the Pakistan government when religious freedom is not upheld and those who speak up for religious freedom are gunned down is tantamount to an anti-Christian foreign policy." The Catholic Church in Pakistan requested that Pope Benedict declare the martyrdom of Shahbaz Bhatti.

At least 20 people, including police officials, were wounded as 500 Muslim demonstrators attacked the Christian community in Gujranwala city on 29 April 2011, Minorities Concern of Pakistan has learnt. During a press conference in Karachi, the largest city of Pakistan, on 30 May 2011, Maulana Abdul Rauf Farooqi and other clerics of Jamiat-Ulema-e-Islam quoted "immoral Biblical stories" and demanded to ban the Bible. Maulana Farooqi said, "Our lawyers are preparing to ask the court to ban the book."

On 23 September 2012, a mob of protesters in Mardan, angry at the anti-Islamic film Innocence of Muslims, reportedly "set on fire the church, St Paul's high school, a library, a computer laboratory and houses of four clergymen, including Bishop Peter Majeed." They went on to rough up Zeeshan Chand, the pastor's son. On 12 October 2012, Ryan Stanton, a Christian boy of 16 went into hiding after being accused of blasphemy and after his home was ransacked by a crowd. Stanton stated that he had been framed because he had rebuffed pressures to convert to Islam.

In March 2013, Muslims attacked a Christian neighborhood in Lahore, where more than 100 houses were burned after a Christian was alleged to have made blasphemous remarks. On 22 September 2013, 75 Christians were killed in a suicide attack at the historic All Saints Church in the old quarter of the regional capital, Peshawar.

On 14 February 2014, Muslims stormed the Church building and attacked school property in Multan. They were led by Anwar Khushi, a Muslim gangster who struck a deal with the local people's spokesperson. They seized the Church property and displaced the people and deprived them of their building.

On 15 March 2015, two blasts took place at a Roman Catholic Church and a Christ Church during Sunday service at Youhanabad town of Lahore. At least 15 people were killed and seventy were wounded in the attacks.

On 27 March 2016, at least 70 were killed and over 340 wounded when a suicide bomber targeting Christians celebrating Easter attacked a playground in Lahore. The Pakistani Taliban claimed responsibility for the bombing.

On 17 December 2017, a bomb killed nine and injured fifty-seven. The Islamic State of Iraq and the Levant took responsibility.

Forced conversions of Christian children are known to occur, and if a child resists, they can be raped, beaten, or bullied.

Every Christian in Pakistan is not safe; his or her life is uncertain. Facts have made it clear that no one—from a Christian minister to a minor Christian janitor—is safe. Every day there are cases about small innocent girls being raped. Few cases are reported, and these few cases are hardly moved to the court. Christian's families are being pressured if they make a case against this crime. To make the situation worse, police are most of the time with these criminals because they are Muslims and have money. Christians in many places are not given food. In many places their glasses and tea cups are separate from Muslims.

I have personally known and met many Christian families where whose girls are being raped. I have seen their pain and sorrow. I have a small daughter, so I understand, know and feel their pain very well. It hurts. And if this pain hurts me, you can imagine how much it hurts them. Recently, a man from Sri Lanka was badly beaten, all his bones were broken, he was insulted, and later a Muslim mob set him on fire.

Years ago, a Christian couple was put into a brick kiln. This woman was pregnant. There were sufferings, sorrows, and persecution that you cannot even imagine that Christians are facing here every day.

Christian's colonies and villages have been burnt. People were burned live, and Muslims were making their videos instead of helping them.

So, this is a reality that Christians are living in pain, sorrow, darkness, hopelessness, uncertainty, and in a certain kind of death every day.

A New Hope

Chapter 5

Impact of this Ministry (Children of the Cross) on Pakistan

Books of Mary Kloska have been instruments to heal, educate, strengthen, and unite many hearts. Miraculously these books have strengthened, healed, and helped people here in Pakistan and even in Afghanistan.

"Violence against Pakistani women begins from young [sic]. Many are raped; sexual assault remains one of the most common crimes in Pakistan.) According to The Human Rights Commission, rape occurs every three hours in Pakistan (excluding the numerous unreported cases); many women are forced into marriages or prostitution or have acid thrown onto them. Some go through honour killings and human trafficking. Girls, unlike boys, are not allowed to play games that can help in speeding up their mental and physical development. If a woman is suspected of having an extra-marital relationship, a common practice is to cut off her nose." (https://nyghihpakistan.weebly.com/females-receive-unfair-treatment.html)

Now in this situation described above you can well imagine that Christian women are always living in a fearful situation. But the books of Mary Kloska and especially her book on *The Holiness of Womanhood* is really healing these young girls and giving them and their families a certain peace of mind and heart.

Articles and videos about these incidents against women and Christian minorities are easily found on social media. This information is just a click away. People are living in pain and tough times.

Children of the Cross is the hope for these wounded people. This ministry is always praying for and with them.

Groups of "Children of the Cross" with their teachers go to the families and pray with them. I have seen with my own eyes that these crying families have felt some peace with these prayers. The prayers of the children have power.

This ministry is not only helping here in Pakistan but also providing peace in Afghanistan, too. And with the favor of Our Lady, it will reach the whole Middle East.

This ministry has given light, life, hope, and peace to people who are living in darkness, hopelessness, and in a certain fear. The book *Out of the Darkness* has brought many people out of their darkness.

This ministry has helped people to boast their missionary spirit. This ministry helped and bore the expenses of two missionaries who went to another province to experience the closeness of God.

Because of this ministry, many conversions have taken place. People from other religions have experienced the power of prayers. Non-Christians have joined us to pray. They have seen and experienced the truth of Christianity. Groups of pray-ers who make up the Children of the Cross are growing in number. But the amazing grace is that in these groups many children have come from other religions. They want to pray with us. This ministry has healed young girls, who are facing a certain death.

It is something graceful that non-Catholic Christian denominations are also attracted to us; they love to pray rosary with us. Here, it would be good to mention that in Pakistan, there is a certain kind of difference among Catholics and other Christian denominations. But this ministry of young children is bringing them to Our Lady as well. The impact of this ministry in Pakistan is life-giving. Wherever people receive unfair treatment, this ministry provides them peace through their faithful prayers.

I remember once I was sitting with a Catholic Priest. I introduced to him to the book *In Our Lady's Shadow: The Spirituality of Praying for Priests*. He was happy and surprised to know that lay people are being encouraged to pray for priests. In my place, it is known that only priests pray for the people, so this priest felt joy that people can remember him and other priests who are in need of prayers. Then later I showed another priest a book *Mornings with Mary (A Rosary Prayer Book)*. So, we both were surprised to see that we do not have simple prayers available in Urdu. I would like to share here that this ministry (these books of Mary Kloska) has enhanced our wisdom and knowledge. It has helped not only lay people but also clergy to grow deeper in our spirituality.

These books promote the well-being of individuals, families, and the community. Continued prayers of these faithful children also lead to a reduction in the incidence of domestic abuse, crime, substance abuse, and addiction. This Ministry (Children of the Cross) makes a significant contribution for the betterment of the society. This Ministry provides a moral compass explaining how we should act in various life situations and especially how we treat each other. It also helps to give meaning to our sufferings. These books explain that sufferings are part of our life. We cannot deny it. We must accept them and turn them into peace and a way to get closer to God. It provides guidance on how to view the world and interact with it. It provides belonging and a sense of community.

People are living in fear and stressful situations. This ministry helps people to define their lives, and thus we can say it gives meaning to our lives. These books help us to deal with the most stressful moments of our lives because it gives us hope to move on. It enables us to avoid depression, and so our lives move more smoothly and in a healthy manner.

And, this ministry of the Children of the Cross is healing people, giving meaning to their lives, consoling them in their grief, providing them their true Christian identity and human dignity, and bringing them closer to God.

Pictures of the different occasions
(Retreats, Seminars, Workshops, Promotions, Launching etc.)

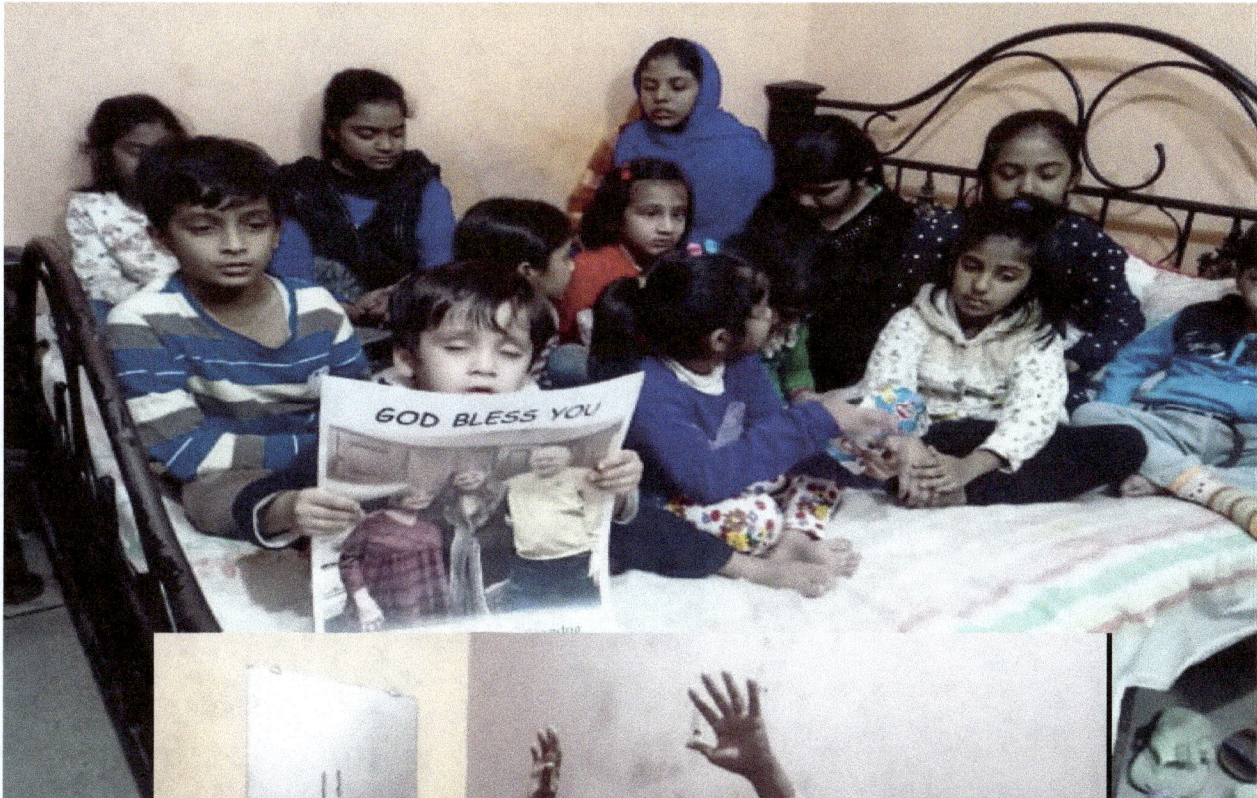

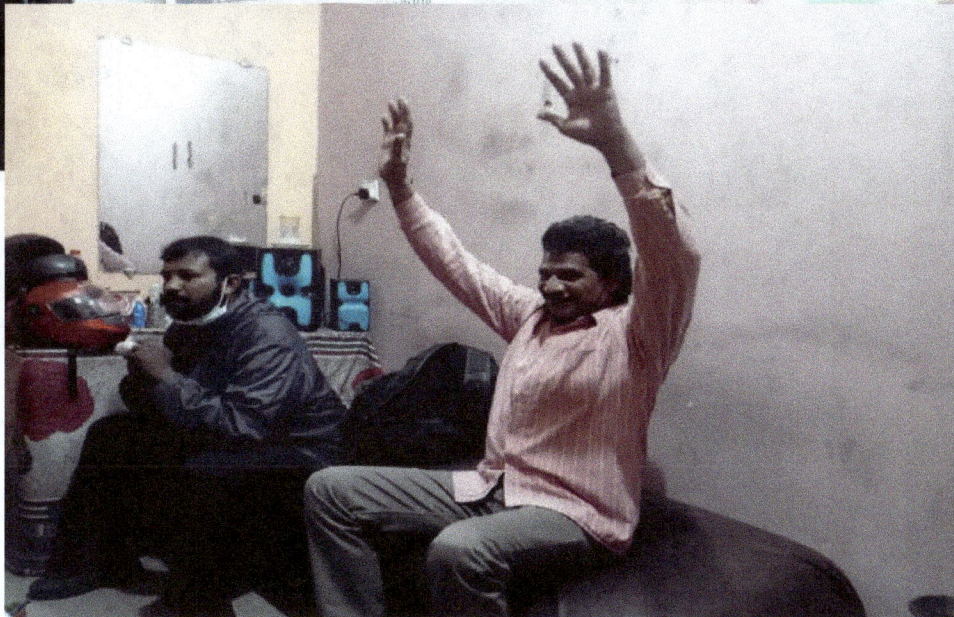

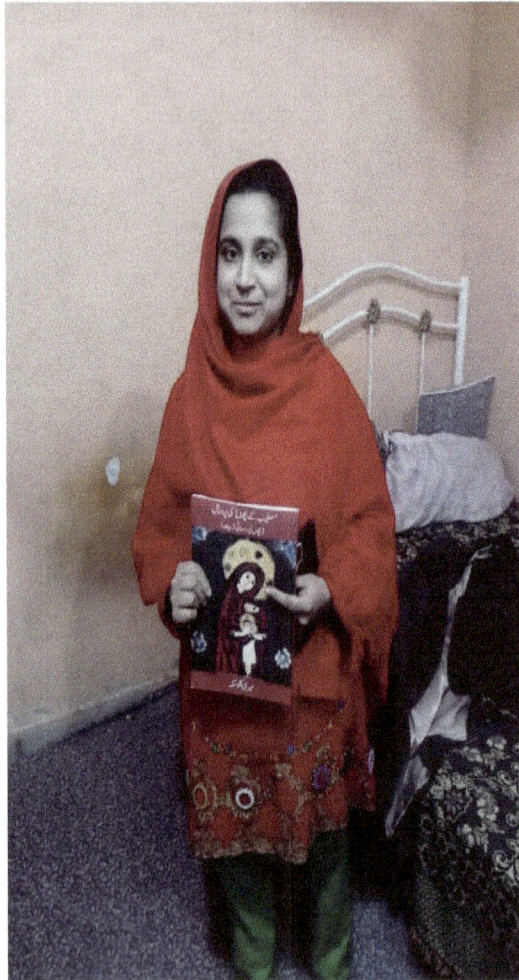 

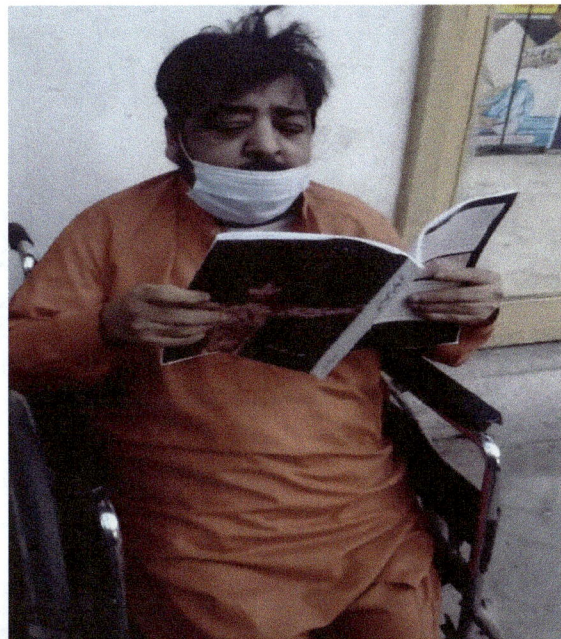

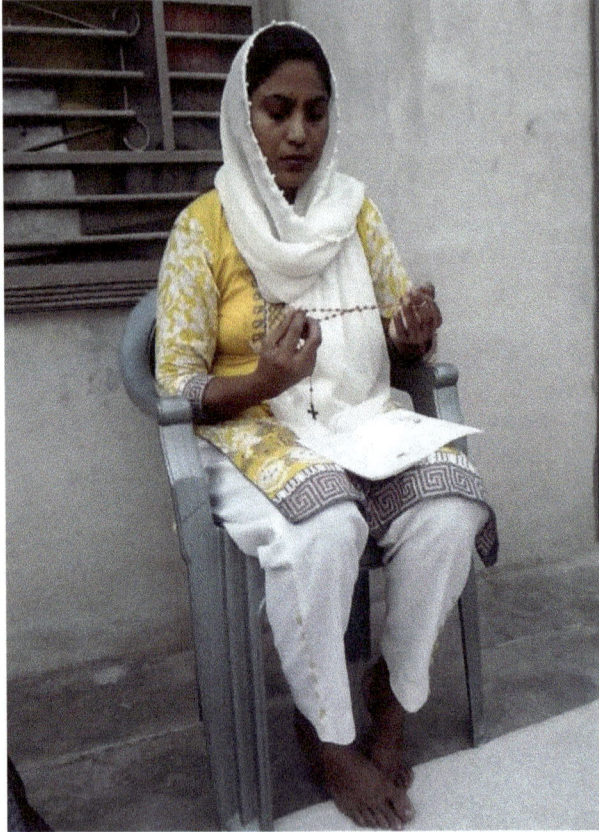

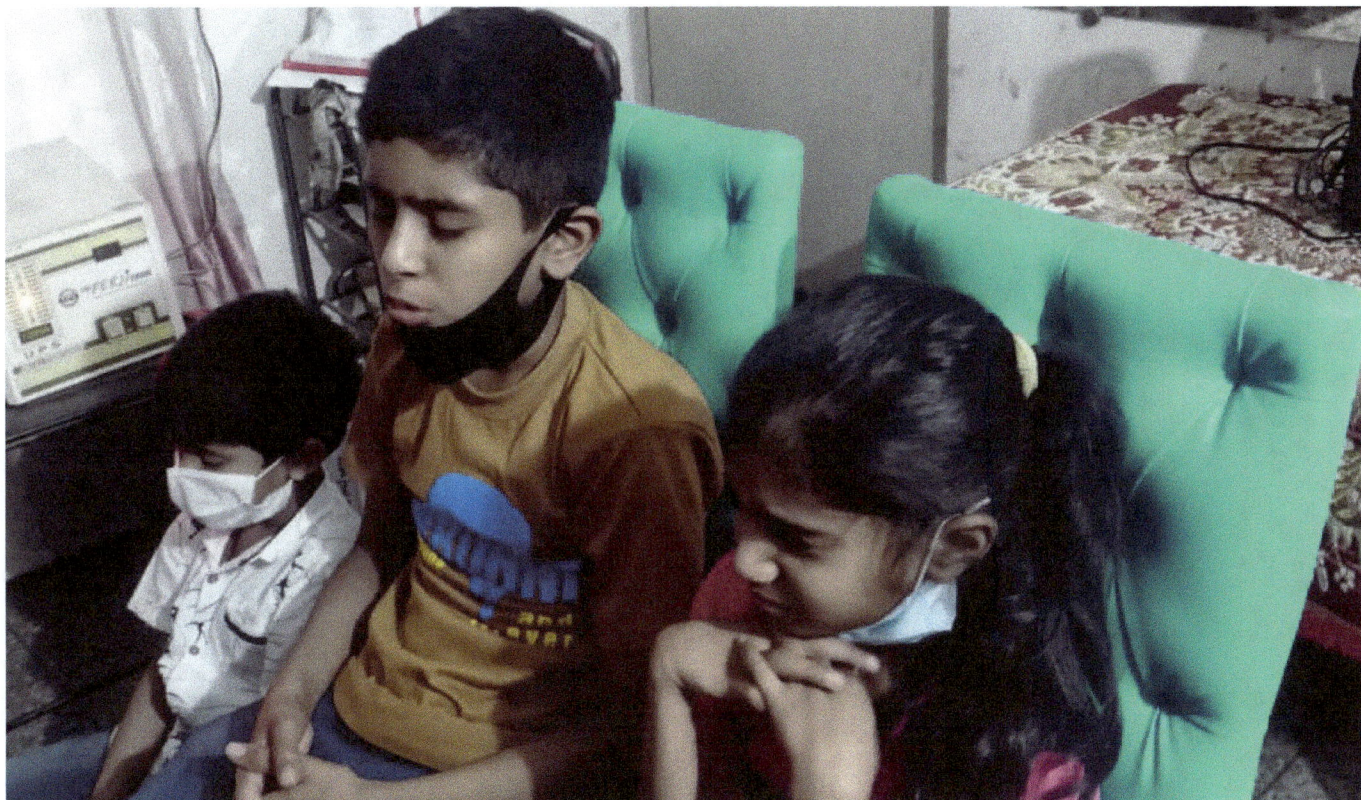

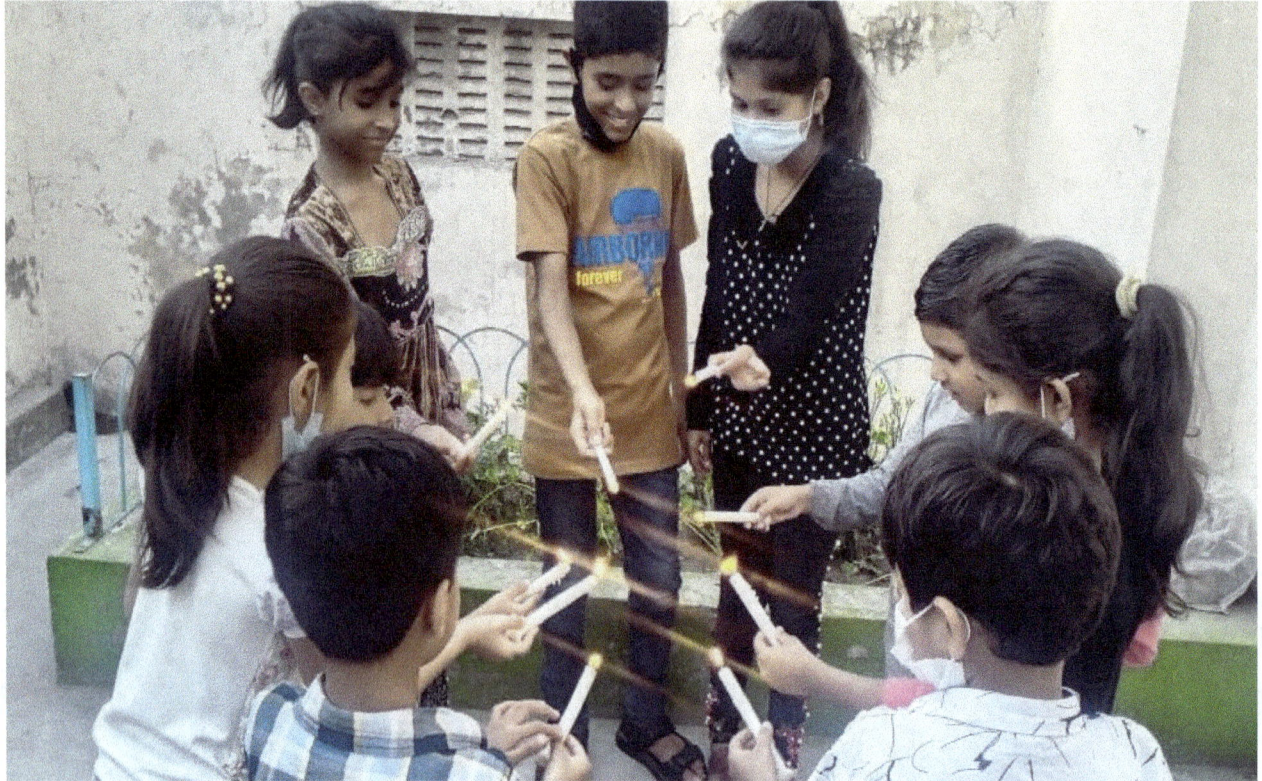

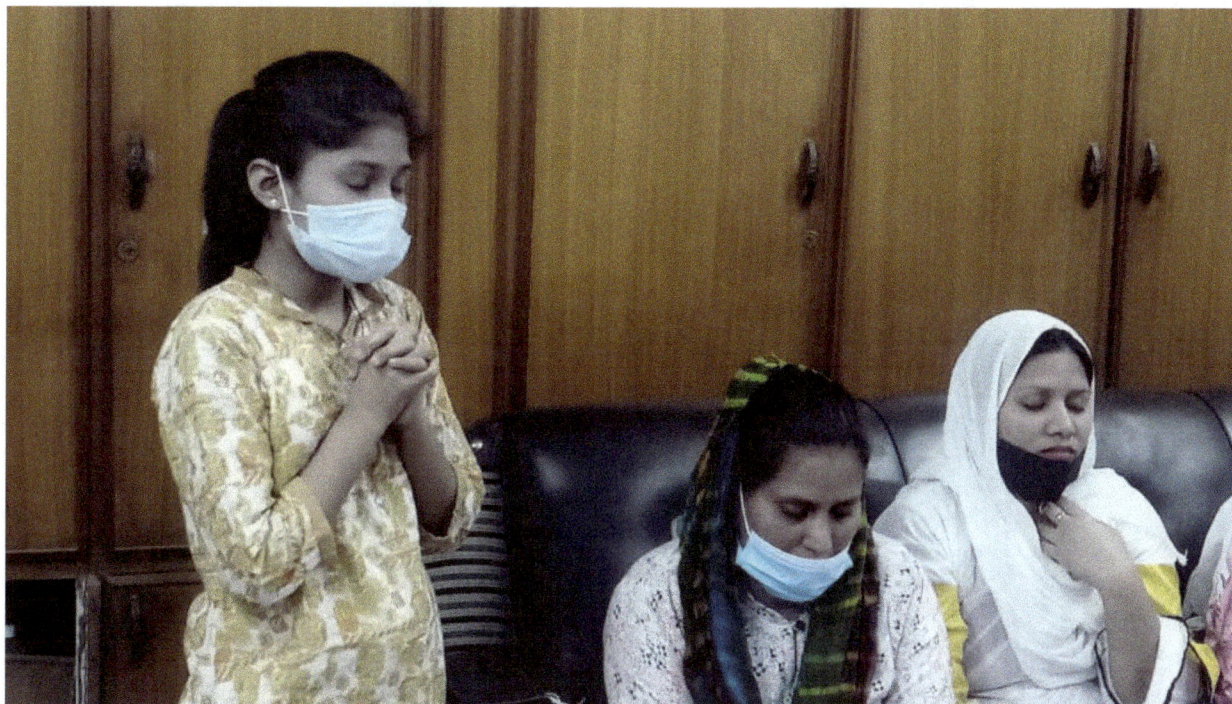

To learn more about Children of the Cross, please visit Mary's website at **https://www.marykloskafiat.com/children-of-the-cross-prayer-groups** and consider making a donation to the continued printing of these books in Pakistan.

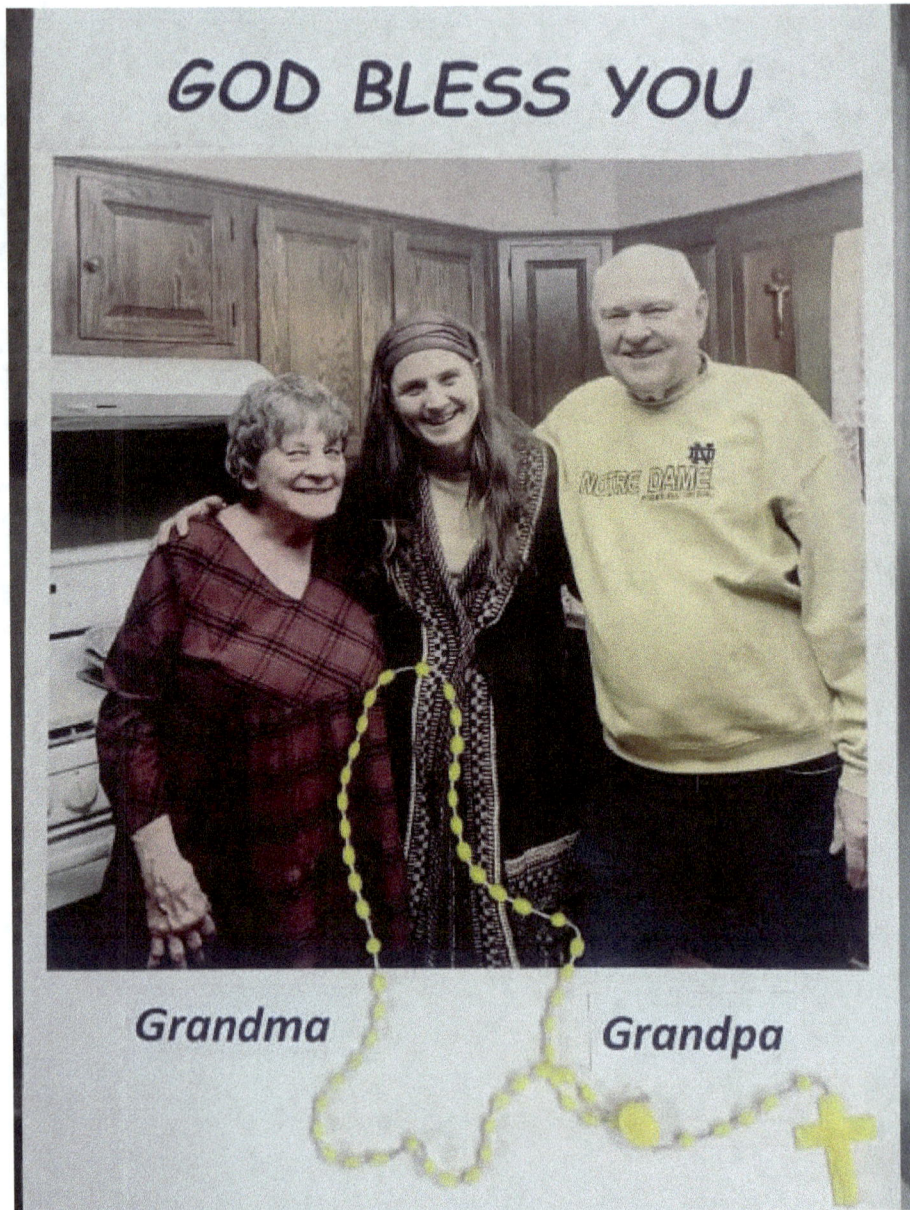

www.ingramcontent.com/pod-product-compliance
Lightning Source LLC
LaVergne TN
LVHW081317060426
835509LV00015B/1568